Marvelous Light

poems

Claude Wilkinson

STEPHEN F. AUSTIN STATE UNIVERSITY PRESS
2018
NACOGDOCHES, TEXAS

MARVELOUS LIGHT. Copyright © 2018 SFA Press

Stephen F. Austin State University Press
PO Box 13007, SFA Station,
Nacogdoches TX. 75962.
sfapress@sfasu.edu

Book design by Emily Townsend
Cover painting titled "Winter Light" by Claude Wilkinson.

ISBN: 978-1-62288-220-5
First Edition

Contents

But ye are a chosen generation, a royal priesthood,
an holy nation, a peculiar people; that ye should
show forth the praises of him who hath called you
out of darkness into his marvelous light.

1 Peter 2:9

We work in the dark—we do what we can—we give
what we have. Our doubt is our passion and our passion
is our task. The rest is the madness of art.

Henry James, "The Middle Years"

I. The Thing That Perches in the Soul

Perfect Submission

Early March has brought a coyote out,
fur ruffling in the breeze
while he trots along
green fringe of a cotton field,
and a mile or so up the road,
a falcon hangs in the morning chill,
her pinion tipped with purpose.

Soon, all redbirds and myrtles,
all our world it seems
will succumb to the sun's beatitudes,
and become showy popinjays.

Once more, petals
will be defenseless against lover bees
pinkly roving from clover
to clover over and over
as new light and buds
duly flood and brighten,
bestowing sight on the blind,
making the lame dance,
and bringing the dumb to praise.

Sweet Tea with Bashō

The woodpecker's knock
wakes all the oldest trees first,
then nodding blossoms.

A fresh dilemma
of buttercups beginning—
stray and unwanted.

Though March twentieth,
dogwoods claim spring hasn't hit
in Mississippi.

New honeysuckle
opens its yellow fountain
and drips golden bees.

Tiresias comes
to mind with thoughts of crushing
two mating crane flies.

The first shaky fawn
stumbles through wine red clover,
also drunk on spring.

Waiting until dark
covers it, a small toad hides
among other stones.

Fireflies have started
to trust the warming night air—
love flashes and waits.

For now, just an elm
feels the owl's sharp, eager clutch—
there's rustling below.

Even stars listen
to check that every cricket
is perfectly tuned.

The Egret Tree

In the past, I have asked for what this may be,
        more faithfully perhaps,
haven't I, for some covenant of intimate favor

        waiting along a byway?
So how then should it be seen, what begins as just
        a blue, late morning crease

between heavy rains, noticing the usual roadside toll
        of dark's itinerant deer
and foolhardy raccoons, reticent miles without towns?

        Now in moments
of determined light on slowly brightening copse,
        such pleasantness,

such absence of profundity like birdsong in autumn,
        is still an ellipsis.
And yet how can that be of something so infinitely finite

        as ripe alluvion
sweeping groves of cypress trees, one in particular
        so thoroughly bleached with egrets

that its evergreen can scarcely be imagined?
        Yet dozens of them
paying me no mind, waiting for water levels to drop,

        and I not truly knowing
what they mean on this route are nonetheless together
        in the suddenness of passing.

What abstractions of holiness we are always asked
        to read and understand
as if in the brevity of even a hundred years

        we might grasp
from where all the starlings one day fall in harmony
        with shadows and leaves,

how we stray through phases of grace.
   But these egrets
in transcendent whiteness appear not to weigh notions

   of good and sin,
and though reverently steady, don't seem thankful for anything other
   than no present threat from above or below.

They are hungry, or tired, or content to have others about.
   Yet stark in their whiteness,
there's never anything to regret or forgive,

   nothing more necessary
than fishing, their brood. None flutter and primp
   like we would expect

in one of Audubon's wild clusters. Instead
   they pose, poised as if
on a scroll for meditation, accompaniment to haiku.

   Nothing in this morning's
static of banked cloud ruffles the nuptial plumes,
   not a rising tide of litter

and duckweed swirled around their roost, nor I
   in my clumsy Keatsian desire
to join their approval of our whole imperfect world.

Mid-May

In the already tight
Midas-grip of pollen,
sunrises stir
from a sapsucker's tapping,
and somewhere no doubt,
spring lambs are falling.

By night, beside
the glycerin works
of fireflies, calls
of frogs and crickets
are like thousands of clocks
being wound.

And who can say
what harassment
that big owl intends,
yonder in the tall sweet gum,
as if perched
on Minerva's shoulder,
woofing nearness,
winking its moons,
before gliding off
through brush?

When it's also time
for covenant to be kept
after a long anniversary,
earth blooms
with cicadas' alien force—

light into dark,
dark into light,
until the moment we have to bear
that first shrill,
empty silence, when
in unison, they just stop singing,
and the rest of our world
resumes.

Something for LaShurn

An arbor of clematis or ivy
greening before a late afternoon storm,
over ice cream, she smiled and quipped,
"It's your treat next time."
The rains came between this
and her asking whether I thought
I'd ever found the right girl.

Perhaps if either of us
at that age had looked up
for a moment and felt something
even remotely ironic or profound
about dark, billowing clouds
intensifying the last gold
of sunlight, I might recall
the essence of what else was said.

But what I save more particularly
is a dream that brought her back
after so many years, her marriage,
and the birth of sons.
Oddly, it begins in Austria,
or it could have been Switzerland
as they are enough alike.

We waltz among dreaming others,
under festive streamers fluttering above,
under a redundantly clear moon,
to Berlioz, Ravel, Strauss,
she and I infallibly together,
so that waking would be
like her betrothal again, leaving
the heartbroken boys of DeSoto County,

like hearing the news again
from my friend who pined for her
through three living wives,
stopping by to tell me

that she was "low sick with cancer"
in Oklahoma or Nebraska
though he wasn't sure which,
so that all the customary words:
in memoriam, elegy, lament—
would seem somehow less than right.

Two Pretty Girls Wave Goodbye to Two Young Boys at a Bus Stop in Edinburgh

I'm trying to remember
if either of the boys
wore a tam-ó-shanter or kilt.
Some of it's lost
among golden spring flowers
that painted my climb
into the Highlands
and misty hillsides
stippled with sheep.

And then there were
the dark choppy lochs
with their many, many white birds
fluttering in the blue above.

What I do recall
isn't any regret over spent youth,
but just a confluence
of humanness, feeling that age
when even the thoughts
about girls' innocent softness,

when the melody
of their names only,
could still be enough
to lift happy, ruddy-cheeked boys
onto a bus and send them
bounding for the upper deck's secrecy
like two wild harts
that had been captured
and released.

Dreams into Paintings, Paintings into Dreams

after paintings by Maxfield Parrish

1. The Garden of Allah

Where shall we turn for prophecy here—
to path softly aglow
rising briefly at the composition's center
before disappearing into luminous viridian,
to the gnarled sienna trunks of great ancient trees,
or to the four stone sentinel urns
looking nearly diaphanous from cast shadows
of branches and leaves,
or constellations of aqua and pink florets
framing, enfolding, overflowing this scene
even to their own glistening image
in a calm foreground pool, or possibly
the two poolside virgins veiled in white,
one sitting tucked and twisted
on such slender wrist, surely asking
girlish questions, while the other
with her back to the rest of bliss,
lies propped on elbow
almost completely lost in her reflection, or to the one
who appears to be their mother
kneeling between the two, her glance
mildly askew as if remembering
how to teach a delicate lesson?
As usual with Parrish's resplendent eyes,
there's no oracle of explanation, merely
a dusting of oddly familiar light
promising always some wonder
that seems good, pleasant, and wise.

2. Wild Geese

Like so many of Parrish's
slender, alabaster maidens
who've somehow perched
among jagged heights,
or beside raging cataracts,
somehow without scab or bruise,
without ruining their virginal tunics,
and without any aid in sight,
this ethereal one arches
from her prone position
on what might seem
an uneasy ledge to us,
except her profile appears blushed
with the kindred rose and violet
brightening mountainside, the same
electric gold about her hair
and sash as surges
through the cliffs like veins.
By whatever she's watching,
her bare arms and legs
have transcended the cold
of altitude. A luminosity
shows her unafraid.
Though to make sense
of the painting's title, we
have to imagine a wedge
of gracefully soaring geese
she's joining well above
her own summit, where the birds
and her spirit become one.

3. Romance

The Knave of Hearts, as it were,
and Lady Violetta have baked tarts together.
Yet in another scene from this drama,
Lady Ursula kneels with hands
covering her face before Pompdebile,
as if confessing some other, fresh indiscretion.

But now why then in heaven's name
should our Knave and Violetta seem to be
so tragically torn on this verandah
even though their moonlight
is still soft enough for embracing?

Aren't the not too distant castles
nestled amongst the mountains
and also bathed in the bluish cast
quite lovely enough for them
to gaze at together?

And why aren't such radiant trees,
those perfect peaks and ridges enough to keep
the Lady from sinking, as if now somehow
diminished, into the faded pink corolla
of a single rose she is holding?

For some reason, I think of the poem,
"In Bertram's Garden," feel the Knave has done
something regrettable, and that however secret,
will not be forgotten, perhaps something
for which I too should apologize.

Or we may imagine all this
has nothing to do with any of our pasts,
that the Lady's head is bowed merely
in sweet adoration, instead that the Knave's
attention upon her as she walks away
is warmed with beautiful truth.

The Blood of Birds

Leviticus warns against consuming
the blood of birds with a promise
of being cut off from the chosen,
like in some way I suppose,
generations of boys being told
never to shoot a mockingbird.
And as far as I know, none of us ever did—
not even Hoolie Sturghill,
who surely would have,
just to see if its blood would be
the shade of ripe plums,
or if there was anything hallowed
in how it would fall
from the grace of holly and elm.
So it's not the spilling of their life
for which I need to be forgiven,
but for the fluorescent goldfinch
lit on a cone of thistle,
the sudden epaulets of a redwing
across cloudless sky, for ending
the quirkiness of nuthatches
and a thrush's optimism.
But what were they to me then except
so many clichés of prettiness?
Anyway, I couldn't have imagined
being under the dull curse
of an earth without birds
no matter how many of them I killed,
nor would any of us have traded the pride
that rose with a perfect aim
to send blue jays
and vermilion cardinals
tumbling ablaze into silence
through limbs over gullies and springs,
until alas, we headed home
from some fresh Elysium,
bringing our brightest sacrifices
for the gods of praise to shower us
with what good shots we were,
and bestow everlasting favor.

Before Waking

There were no cygnets with it
in this brief dream,
no brilliantly lit water
daubed with anything as usual
as the falling colors
of sweet gum or maple,
no spangled glades
nor Hughes's lunacy of swifts
dipping through quilted skies
nor Hopkins's cherished finches.

But in the limbo that holds us
just before waking,
almost like a solar prominence
my white, solitary swan
glided in total darkness,
its neck and crown as resolute
as a cello's fingerboard and scroll.

Midmorning finds me
still pondering this, now
nearly a hundred miles along,
passing dashes of beige leaves
between Greenwood and Grenada,
and as yet, the vision is only that—
one mute swan
surrounded by nothing but black.

After Vaughan Williams's *Pastoral Symphony*

Notes become
so like a harmony
of larks
perched on staffs
in silhouette,
but at least still
of our earth, then rise
alas toward heaven
and dissolve
in silver light.

Waiting for the Train from Holyhead

Monopolized by those bright,
otherworldly Welsh names of places
popping up and skating across
our timetable screen, I didn't even notice
how that white pigeon had landed—
landed with only one foot, I mean.
Now almost a martlet, it was still handsome,
sprinkled with rose and gray.

Of course, my first thought
was that some naughty cat
had nearly caught it
and this was the damage done,
before two young locals
sharing my bench also saw it.

One remarked on the possibilities.
Though his friend said
it was a kind of fungus they got
that starts as a lump on the toe
and just eats and eats
until the whole foot is gone.

"I was wondering about that,"
I nudged in, and asked the expert
how the birds fared, if they could take off
and perch and survive okay.

He assured me that they managed.
But after a moment,
thinking further on it, I asked,
"What if the fungus claims the other foot too?"
He looked puzzledly at me,
down at the pavement,
over to the bird, and offered,
"Then, I guess they're screwed."

Spring

after a painting by Ernest Lawson

Moments such as this was, circa 1900,
are so brilliant in their blossomed air
drizzled with pinks and reds,
with flourishes of green
and an aurora of goldenness,
that jeweled mist now clearing
by a panpipe of breezes,
opening the shady slope of violets,
and a brook too, shimmering like flowers.

Yet before the land's animals
have wandered up through
distant teal blue trees, before
a little glowing house has awakened,
everywhere is soft and still.
A lattice of scribbled willows
arcs across the foreground,
and a hint of white pickets
bridge the quiet run of water.

Everything about the scene
echoes our breach between
memory and remembrance—
that is, dabs and swirls bless us
in a cusp of enchanting seconds
before longing or something draws us closer
to where we can see only
muddled splotches of color
and the inevitable cracks of time.

After Watching *Paris Blues*

I dreamt in French the other night—
young in those shabby hotels
with Newman and Poitier,
suffering the happy tomcatting
all night long into smoky morning riffs
of drums, trumpets, and saxophones
that searched the streets like lost pets—
none of us ever blessed with more
than a couple hours of quiet.

Skip to the scene of the cool, blue
bohemian girl feeding salad
to some rabbits in hutches
on the roof of a tenement while a party
spills through rooms below, and whom
sleep cast as a pretty, dark-haired regret
with this Parisian-sounding name
from Vicksburg, Mississippi.
For my tumultuous love interest,
I think it may have been
an Algerian hostess that I once met
at the Musée d'Orsay on a spring afternoon.

Though in the dream, it didn't matter
so much whether musicians' jazz fell
or soared like in the movie.
It was that everything else was so filled
with these unbearable freedoms again,
as a time when all possibilities
seemed lodged in one's heart, when
even such hazy chaos as this
felt like nothing but light.

Release

In an old movie on the other evening,
           Brits were scrambling to get
their hands on a new bombsight, weaponry
           that would wreck the Germans

and all their fleet, from which I eventually turned
           to come upon an actor
recalling a ceremony he'd once seen in Japan—
           a ceremony also borne of the notion

that the nature of war is to obliterate the other.
           On the movie's silvery bright day,
the bombing test had gone smashingly
           in that they seemed to slip

through the clouds as a practiced glissade,
           or like orderly children
in a perfect row, when one by one by one
           they leapfrogged from line,

then plowed across the countryside.
           And we were to concede
that exaltations of larks were missed in their nests
           and the blue scent of spruce

would have been unsinged, that in its time
           this too could be thought
a good idea as were those noble-sounding
           slave ships, *The Rainbow*,

The Solomon, The Hannibal of London, or as were
           the Auschwitz and Majdanek ovens,
as was that utter stillness up to the very pause before
           Hiroshima left in a firestorm from heaven.

The actor spoke of a slow, soft, enraptured anthem
           played while many stood or sat,
hushed in a kind of reenactment until its last note
           just thirty seconds before

Armageddon would have touched, in which nothing
        but silence fell, until a morning bell
rang at 8:15, until that famous explosion of wings,
        some thousand white "peace" doves

being released, spraying into sky
        a wounded calligraphy,
like an incalculable cipher of spirits
        rising.

Buzzard's Luck

> "Hope" is the thing with feathers—
> That perches in the soul—
> —Emily Dickinson

As further evidence
to the strength in faith
or our faith
in chance,
while once passing
lush pastureland
grazing some
of the sleekest Angus cows
you've ever seen,
even here,
despite mild blue skies,
at the heart
of spring,
there was a convocation
of Grim Reapers
as steady
as dirges
lining limbs
in the heights
of two bone-dead trees.

II. *Summer Nights*

Learning to Swim

The pond somewhere,
placid yet glistening
with promises of buoyancy,
holding us perfectly aloft
like a bird on the wing
is what each of us dreamt of,
what each of us awakened for
till his time finally came.

In spite of bitter legends from kin
about waiting cottonmouths
and boys our age
being swallowed by sinkholes,
we followed water routes,
finding our way through rich persimmon
or loblolly pine.

Then mystified there
at its fetid indifference,
hailed among the dobsonflies,
each of us shed his mortality,
felt glances of comparison,
sand and mud ooze between toes
in those giddy steps to brotherhood.

Our hierarchy ranged
from those who could only teach
how to float and dog paddle
to the two or three
who stroked like Tarzan.

And when the anaphora
of instruction started, we latched our eyes,
breathed without rhythm,
fell for that cool netherworld
time and again
till as suddenly as failing,
we were no longer groping
for what was possible anymore
but lifted to another realm,

which like everything else—
the swath of afternoon sun,
a startled heron's harsh alarm—
was becoming bone of our bone
and flesh of our flesh,
our new birth

where we began to understand
the downward thrust of the palms,
that the kick should come
mainly from one's hips,
and where afterward in vain,
we tried to wash disobedience
from behind ears, along hairlines,
before wading clear for home.

Not then of course,
but now for some reason,
I try to imagine how and why
anyone first did this,
Adam perhaps bobbing a young Cain,
and later the favored Abel,
till finding water's grace,
when each one could move beyond
the caring shallows
out on his fallible own.

Early Morning on the B Line from Vero Beach to Orlando after a Poetry Festival

On the road before sunrise,
so none of us were citing
Homer, Keats, or Dickinson
during the drive to catch my flight.
Only after I'd asked, did Sean
and Jens mention the anaconda
they had found once
in Sean's cattle pasture.

From time to time,
someone spotted the height
of egret whiteness
crossing daybreak's blaze
or a runty marsh deer
sprung from her rushes
or a flock of wild turkeys
on the shoulder interrupted.

In heavy, unexpected traffic, Jens
talked of his old job at an abattoir,
how they cleaned and sent
the best pigskins
for making footballs.
Then Sean recalled how skillfully
his own son had eviscerated
their dead heifer for autopsy
a couple of weeks ago.

And as the lengthening string
of brake lights lingered,
Jens remembered a similar moment
some thirty years before
when a flower child, his hair
flowing from under
a red bandanna,
strode past lanes of stalled cars
as buck-naked as he pleased.

Though all of it passed over me
like sand over glass.
I wanted too much to know more
about a thing that could
swallow any of us whole,
as it had in Eden,
if my friends witnessed
some epiphany in the snake's
ashen scales or those jeweled eyes,
whether his tongue was split
with a few dry morsels of truth
and many delicious lies.

William's Garden

On the morning in question,
I could hear raucous crows up to no good,
after my neighbor's roasting ears again
like in an old-time cartoon.
Who knows? Maybe he'd simply had it with deer
keeping every pea vine stripped,
cutworms plus terrapins always sampling
his finest tomatoes in spite of an electric fence,
and late-night raids by armadillos
boring through all his ripe cantaloupes.

Maybe the crows and he were without prescience
or empathy for what each other would soon lose—
he a young stepson in an accident
on a dark, wild highway a few miles from home,
and the crow its mate for life—
when he stamped off through glistening dew
to get his trusted Remington 12-gauge
that he'd used last spring on a big bull snake
suddenly piled under the shed.

Because I only heard the shot
and since William is no poet,
I image the bird hurtling through precious air,
a glossy, rumpled bloom,
in suspended moments as if a still life
hung by one gristly, extended leg from thread
tacked to a neutral background,
it cawing for vendetta, then plumping
among rows of freshly turned earth.

The rest becomes the stuff of myths,
as for a month at least, the dead bird's mate
held vigil in a near pin oak, seething
for William only to come out each day,
then lighting on him with doubled fury
like any of Phineus's Harpies might.

But now in dandelion quiet, the garden,
without squash or radishes or turnips anymore,
has lain fallow for a long while,
and though deer, rabbits, and even a few crows
probably still come from time to time,
they just come for no reason I suppose.

Maine Surf, 1948

after a *Saturday Evening Post* cover by John Falter

From mauve horizon
and iron-blue undulations,
a golden crest of ocean
bursts to brilliant surf, into
softer hues where three
among our scene's
nine rosy swimmers
find themselves
this fine August day.

More daring bucks
are naturally out farther
than the bald but still
well-muscled man
wading through a crash of white,
his pate kissed
with one highlight,
and all of them careless
of who's looking on.

Neither do the five women
notice our gaze.
They are safely in shallows,
in various stages of experience and play,
wearing modestly flattering suits
and donning or removing bathing caps
for perfect hair upon return to earth
there in this rare,
wonderful life.

High Noon, 1949

after a painting by Edward Hopper

Whether it is so or not,
his art appears bound
with the melancholy of autumn.
Though this work, in spite
of his bleached, crackling grass,
in spite of the long shadows
and faltering radiance, I'd say
is at latest the end of July
or the beginning of August.

It's just that the fresh house's curtains
look opened for any chance
of a breeze and that the horizon
is still a summery enough blue.

In the doorway, stands
his own golden-haired wife
gazing into the swell of noon,
as she similarly would a year from this—
next time wearing a pink housedress
and hair wound in a bun—
staring past the glow of generic trees,
into morning from a bay window,
desperately greeting the day,

and as she would, some decade later,
again lost in her portal of oblivion,
or maybe only nonchalance,
holding a cigarette while sun through nearby glass
falls upon her naked body, slants across
an unmade bed, which some
have tried to find the Annunciation in.

But it's here in the noonday scene,
that her expression for once
seems to border genuine pleasure.

A manganese blue duster is slit
down the front of her ampleness,
not for us but to welcome the light,
yes, for the warm, gratifying light.

Here, I can even see Hopper himself,
though not visibly in the picture
but a part of it all the same,
inside, before he begins it, leaning
on a sofa arm, over dark coffee
and the last of the season's
good strawberries, considering
her eventual pose, for a while content
in his feverish despair.

Reunion

And here they all are again,
at least those among the living,
casting smiles to show
sharp remarks which pricked
well beyond teenage days
are close to being forgotten.

After bearing one cross
or another for so long,
jokers and clowns seem almost sedate,
and bullies not nearly so big or fierce,
in fact, somewhat wasted away.

But I mostly notice what's become
of our girls—the bookish and soubrettes,
those who left early to be grown,
married, and the ones whose stars
quickly flared then faded—
so unrecognizable except for her,
even now in soft,
though less divine light.

Coming toward me as I feared,
the once beautiful-bodied girl
will ask if I remember her
through the frown lines
of children and divorce, through wisps
of silver twirled at her temples.

Yet what would I do but
look at her longer than necessary
as if to mean, no I don't remember
if while leaving the dance, night birds
were calling, nor luminous moon
catching a boy from another school
and you sprawled across the seat
of his green Torino under gently bending poplars,
the cloying magnolia blooms; as if to mean,

I never hushed my steps
to watch the two of you, but so as
not to break your callow rhythm,
to slip behind my steering wheel
and drive toward home
for the next forty years.

Summer Nights

after photographs by Robert Adams

To begin, we peep through a pitch-black eclipse into open drapes of a 1980s wood-paneled room with stone fireplace and part of a Barbizon scene visible atop the mantelpiece. And though all else we can see are a white sofa back and woman's dark coiffure dully leaning on the left hand of her gently bent arm, we believe she's by herself, lost in some novel's impossible romance. Since she looks to be, or to have been a mother and wife, depending on how we want this story to go, we must convince our eyes that at least another is inside out of view, going about a nightly routine of the last twenty-plus years, that the woman is at ease after a better than average day, and then, turn away.

*

Perhaps earlier she visited this amusement park, still lit but vacant now, save one figure appearing to check that all is well, that no stray children have hidden amid the fun, before extinguishing the ferris wheel, merry-go-round, and finally, orbiting canopies of a paratrooper ride as bright and lifeless as Jupiter's moons against a bank of roiling clouds.

Along the route, trees such as these three seem a family of guardians. Though the foreground is so dark for catching sight of anything, miles and miles away, tangent to the soft line of mountains, beads of light welcome all still up and about.

*

Summer in eastern Colorado too has sewn its black-eyed Susans along this road through hushed farms, yet a couple of lights are on, so that one passing may wonder, since all else is dark, if they were the brightness of affliction, if they were someone's only comfort, or otherwise one could gaze at the calm, not quite cirrus, neither cumulus pattern of clouds and consider any number of pleasant things like the bel canto of birds and crickets. And then too, there's all that stuff that Blake once said about the evening star and angels and love and radiance and a lake and dew, the new day coming, and how much livelier the same flowers will look soon.

*

Asphalt narrows, crests toward twilight where a lone household's autos haven't yet been garaged, where a streetlight's starburst ignites. The middle ground offers silhouettes of a few signs and trees, and further on the horizon, one or two more signs and what well may be a few more trees.

The lot across from cookie-cutter houses is overgrown, so that one questions the passions of a younger generation. Why hadn't there been a smart schoolboy keeping the grass cut with some shiny dream in mind. Inside each place, a room is lit, probably for similar dinners, to watch the same TV show. But backlighting the scene is a mysterious glow, like something remarkable being born.

*

Here one could cherish such an hour as this in this grove, off road for a spell, sitting hidden by shadows, or out in spots of moonlight. For all practical purposes, the sky is wonderfully bright, and the community glimpsed through their arboretum must appear like a star-of-Bethlehem to moths far and near being dispatched from velvet cases.

What good does it do to try and fathom the oncoming car's purpose for being out, whether it's an assignation that the driver is up to, when spheres of light dance blindingly around headlamps, across the road even into the many spangled plants?

*

That yard's flowers, which from the distance, seem to be foxglove or snap-dragons, are caught in a crossfire of light. Stout wires sing overhead of the afternoon's cheerleader practice, a recipe for broccoli and rice casserole, what the doctor really said.

On this dark road, one can only imagine crowns of trees, a circumspect badger that may have waddled across, the haunting whisper of an owl's wings, all things beyond the shoulder's dip. But at least, should another be driving ahead of you, only too slowly, the stripe along here allows for him to be legally passed—a kind of unnamable relief.

*

Who was it, if anyone, who once said, *Everything is hinged on symmetry*, or *Symmetry is akin to peace?* Anyhow, similar aphorisms could arise from witnessing these far, alien orbs of light which almost sit on the tops of brush fringing an empty parking lot, and this one illuminated tree centered before the curtain of night, under a crescent's glory.

Village above a shaded ravine, upswept clouds and the monastic look of the sky—it all smacks of El Greco, except in Colorado rather than Spain. If the little hotel is lucky, it may have two or three weary guests back from the coffee shop at this late hour, who may be watching an old black and white movie in which a crude rocket hurtles through deepest space, or else they are squinting into dark caverns of ancient Greece where a loinclothed hero battles a many-headed beast. And now, perhaps, at last nearing sleep.

*

Even nightingales passing would wonder who lives in this duplex with its falling number 11339 slanted by the door. But now is not our time to know, as curtains are drawn for bed. There are odd picket shutters framing second-story windows. A miniature cascade of lights sparkles from one room. The entry is one of those generic, aluminum jobs meant mainly to keep out flies. Enclosing their small yard, at least the corner that can be seen, is a makeshift wooden fence. Someone has started and stopped cradling the lawn with brick. One inside could be a jilted girl from Affinity, West Virginia, who moved out west to set the screen afire, back only this far east toward home, who of late, listens to Coltrane, and most days now, handles the early-bird shift alone. Perhaps one is a late middle-aged man who enjoys Parcheesi, of whom others usually begin, "Think what you will," when describing him. Or maybe neither of these.

*

Thoreau would likely have more to say about some divine throng of life awaiting its blessing of light inside these two gnarled trees—so much more than we can actually see.

A streetlight tells that someone has been watering the yard. Houses are pretty much dark with no other signs of life except that there are houses and manicured grass and a white mailbox whose flag may have been raised earlier today before the postman came.

At most, one light is on in each house up and down this anytown street. But what looks to be a brightened field for play in a corner of the night beams from a mile away, so some may be cringing as their sons or daughters run to steal bases, while other neighbors' pickups and campers are harbored at home, safe.

*

Tonight, the corner stop sign near 10843 stands lawfully quiet. There may be nothing as dissonant as an argument brewing, blaming another for really messing up this time. True, there are a couple of lights on in rooms where no one may be using them, and the shrubbery could stand some pruning. Other than that though, roof shingles seem straight, bricks properly pointed, and the siding is in good shape.

*

The whole scene is Americana framed, from a huge tree that has held the fort for Heaven knows how long, to peeling clapboards in all their Rockwellian glory. Once upon a time, it may have been an Eisenhower house. Now, who knows? Only a small Babylon of potted palm and tendrils of hanging vine can be seen through the window, but there are probably vases of yellow and red tulips or pink tea roses on shelves all around.

*

Lush, rampant leaves overhang a weedy, moonlit sidewalk which is curiously inviting in spite of engulfing dark. In passing, one might wonder about the place's feeling of abandonment, or merely be still for a while, and marvel in absolute quiet.

Pavement has been silvered by sprinklers or an evening shower. Though we can't yet see them, we expect the houses all to have dormers and that somehow, most of the marriages last. Gilded by streetlight, the next intersection says, "Fifth" and something. There's a plain stop sign, trusty mailbox, and the trees are certainly thriving.

*

Dead end, the flimsy fence and utter dark explain. *If you've wound up here at this off-the-beaten lane of tumbleweed and gravel, you're successfully lost. Somewhere you missed an important turn. You must now turn back and head another way, unless that is, you want to trespass, unlash my easy gate.*

Two towering white poles rain light over a paddock, which for some reason looks like an image that a minimalist poet might've described having come across the one horse still grazing well past dark and a few dots of light scattered about the countryside before a range of misted mountains.

*

If it's not passed too quickly, one could guess about this solitary tree—the soundness of its rugged bark, why it's still barren this late into the everywhere fecund season.

Oh, so it's not the interrupted stare of a spooked raccoon—just the glitter of refuse strewn along the roadside, catching someone's high beams among much darker things.

This sky, this field are too calm for there to be enmity anywhere—anywhere in the world. Even the meekest of travelers here would seem to be shepherded through darkness, and spreading trees are like Eden again for pendulums of wrens.

The patchy dirt road may prove a long way round since mostly what can be seen are a latticework of wires crisscrossing dark hills, the small sign jabbed into a corner of tall grass, and a couple of plots where someone may build in time.

No matter what's going on elsewhere, there are still places such as these, where by a certain time of night, all souls have fallen asleep, illuminations may barely be seen, and a glossy weed's shadow inches across an empty street.

*

In the sunlight, one wouldn't have noticed in a field of tasseled weeds how this particular tree twists like a serpent or a stormy life, but with moon finding bows and bends . . . but in the low music of night. . . .

Are those aspens there, shimmying in the wind? Must be. What else could stand out like something golden against such velvety black sky? What else would rejoice so from the slightest touch of air?

There's still enough light along here so that the verge and a few posts can be seen. If there's a clever little boy still awake, remembering one of his readers, in the car whose headlights are rounding the pine-tufted hill, he's already exclaimed that it looks just like a napping dinosaur's back.

Such a molten pool of light glows in this valley below the Rockies that even through the pergola of branches and everything happening in the acres between, one's only thought is likely to be: *What on earth this late would still be that bright?*

*

Over the fence, across someone's pasture, there seems to be a barn or a shed. It's too dark to tell. There are the clouds, of course, and out there beyond them, the bow of Orion. There are the shadows stretching past their groves, but as for roan ponies and ambling cattle and happy rabbits lazing in a wave of clover, and a farmer waking to check the sky for rain, and his contented wife going out to fetch fresh eggs from under warm hens in the bliss of early morning, for this we'll have to wait for the faith of day.

Such a field of ephemera, as the next moment isn't promised to any dandelion. And what of the way that the moon shows them off, beholding their sylphid texture, their nearly incredible form?

That crag seems to be waiting for the right traveler to climb it—never mind the stinging kiss of saplings, the startling and being startled, the wild uncertainty of every blind step.

*

Something was here once. Maybe there still is, and that's the reason for all the wires strung over hardscrabble seized with scrubs and weeds. This far from a city, shadows cover most everything like deep, jagged holes, but there's still just enough light to see a cloistered roofline.

Something is written on the cliff yonder, like that "Hollywood" greeting in California, whereas this says, "80" or "60" or "90" or maybe even "GO," and something else in smaller, indiscernible script above. This late, it hardly matters. Still, it would be nice to know.

Behind those luminous pines side by side like ancient columns, the sky is so beautifully thick with promise that one could spend the rest of the night, the rest of a life here waiting for whatever it is to happen.

There's something in the steepness along here, in the mood of the air, the hum of the road, how the bend is curving soon toward dawn, some place well-known.

*

From this view now, even the mountains seem more manageable, somehow less, for whatever that's worth. Thumbnails of landmarks appear. Arteries of light meander into clearings as proof of others up, getting through it with a scratchy gramophone's coloratura, while someone elsewhere is putting the cat outside, and another is likely changing a diaper under a sampler that reads, "Home, Sweet Home."

Snowy Egret Flies over Parched Mississippi Field

Whose juxtaposition is this
        white origami promise
                floating as softly
                        as a child's paper plane

over sprinklings of rose mallow
        along the ditches,
                in a grayish blue delta breeze
                        perhaps clotted with some relief

of brief afternoon rain?
        And why now
                this somnambular hearkening
                        to the wild plum delirium of youth,

and my new longing
        for Vermont or Maine
                as I drive past
                        acre after acre of sunbaked crops,

meeting the occasional rusty pickup
        struggling behind its Confederate tag?
                Whose questions are these
                        that drift and set upon us

down long highways,
        under such otherwise barren skies
                but for this solitary thing
                        tucked into its looping flight,

of a mind bent
        on one perfect cypress knee
                where the whole of life
                        may be spent?

Deus ex Machina

Many days into any kind of drought,
whether lost faith or drying riverbed,
god from machine seems the only way out.

While the ospreys and quick kingfishers scout
for their food in prayer, waiting to be led,
many days into any kind of drought

begins to weaken resolve and feed doubt,
so that birds scoop fish now, swimming or dead.
God from machine seems the only way out

as all the hungry flocks careen about
like Israelites needing to be fed.
Many days into any kind of drought

causes the most obedient and stout
to believe as ancient Greeks who once said,
god from machine seems the only way out.

Yet certain ones stay on their sober route,
following the heart rather than the head.
Many days into any kind of drought,
god from machine seems the only way out.

Morning, Catskill Valley

after a painting by George Inness

When an unbelieving
poet and I spoke
of our dearest painters,
I mentioned
that I loved the way
Inness used color,
to which he said
he never thought of him
as a colorist.

But that's not at all
what I meant—
not his way with color
like you might expect of Miró.
I meant, take for example,
his *Catskill Valley*, the way
fields blend into an Eden of green;
I meant, the way you feel reborn
when you consider
the subtle yet sudden
blood and gold oaks,
those purple-robed
background hills;

what I meant was
how can you not trust
in the certain blue sky,
his brightness of clouds
lofted about, or a piebald cow
slaking her thirst
from the mirror
of a cooling stream?

The herdsman's
scumbled harmony
and slabs of olive gray stone become
such a peaceable kingdom
that Heaven could be like this
is what I mean.

Meadow Flowers (Goldenrod and Wild Aster)

after a painting by John Henry Twachtman

Like a gate to Paradise,
illumined as how
fluttering angels might appear,
the meadow seems misty
while at the same time
impossibly bright.

But there looks to be
hardly any way into
such purity of color,
through the many layers
of lavender and yellow
And yet a few days
before my father passed,
he shouted for my sister
to come quickly to his bedside.

"Haven't we found
a new way of living?"
he asked her.
When she gathered herself
and after being asked again,
not knowing what he meant,
she merely said, "No."

Though he insisted,
"Yes, I think we've found
a new way of living!"
and went on to tell her
about an abundance
of wondrous flowers
he was seeing.

Some years later,
when another sister
brought it up,

I asked if she thought
it had something to do
with all the strong medicine
he'd been taking.
She thought not, rather that
he was catching
glimpses of heaven.

Wouldn't that
be something though,
if there weren't
the glittering cities
and twenty-four karat streets
thrumming with harp concertos—
no souls tipping diadems
or flouncing in long robes,
just the eternity
of a second-chance earth
flushed with asters
and clusters of goldenrod?

Wouldn't we then
become like the flowers too,
our former sufferings
blown from us as no more
than light pollen
into morning air?

For this no doubt,
we would want to let go,
braced by the faith of flowers
among those last, cold moments
before being whisked into a valley
of lemon lilies, or perhaps
blessed with the surety
of wild rose and camellias.

III. *Half Past Autumn*

Half Past Autumn

after photographs by Gordon Parks

1. American Gothic, 1942

He'd been told by a Mr. Stryker
to turn his lens rather than his back
on the country's bigotry.
Enter Ella Watson, as always, in what's best
of her poor wardrobe, from
her cubbyhole full of makeshift
and even poorer grandchildren, come
to another day's char at the FSA.
Softened Stars and Stripes hanging
vertically against the background wall
still clash sharply with Ella's polka-dot dress.
Before her, all we can see
are her broom's slow curve,
and slightly out of focus,
a mop's tussled braids.
Just as the couple in Grant Wood's *Gothic*,
a gaunt woman pictured from crown to waist,
her short hair lightly straightened,
graying, and swept to one side,
searches us in her spectacled stare—
just as solemn as Wood's model's,
but alone, and without the smart cameo
to spruce up her collar,
or behind her, however humble,
a dreamy white gable of home.

2. Storm, Atlantic Ocean, 1942

With so little brightness
separating the firmament,
it looks as if it might have
between the second and third day,
before the man and the garden
and all hell broke loose,
except for a buoy
tilting in foaming crests, except
for the distant cottage or lighthouse
on a misty slip of land
being whipped by cloudbursts,
and except for two birds'
diminutive silhouettes
plunging under heavy gusts.
In the foreground,
other new signs of earth—
stones and the like—emerge.
Still more wondrous
than the turbulent seas
testing their young strength
against every possible boundary,
is that almost beyond our imagining,
some supreme orchestration,
for the moment could keep
that trace of gulls aloft in this,
and focus any such Euroclydon,
and perfectly meter
the darkness and light.

3. Abandoned House in Augusta, Maine, 1944

There is a quiet
we can almost touch
in banked snow and the idle thicket,
as clouds roll across the edge
into our thought.
No one is there to tell us
if that august foreground tree
had been skinned by the flash
of an April storm, or where on it
a young couple joined their names
inside a crude valentine.
Who beside thee
can still recall
maple-filled mornings,
nights with crying children,
all the items of waning?
The dark door and shutters
seem permanently closed,
yet we know cold
wheezes its way
through chimney and sash
like a last, sharp breath.

4. Hercules Brown, Somerville, Maine, 1944

A tarnished hurricane lamp
hangs next to his head.
Hunched toward us a bit,
he's posed before clustered hutches
of age-old remedies like Luden's and Ex-Lax,
a comb display with its faded sketch
of a well-groomed man,
and something else advertised
as "refreshing, delicious," to be
"enjoyed by the whole family," served anytime.
His tattered newsboy cap,
the stubbled, rugged chin,
a calm, marbled pipe
casting its slender shadow
from thin, windburned lips
down his grungy jumper,
that most of the many odds and ends
sell for less than fifty cents—
everything so appropriate,
even his gaze, which seems
to be wondering of the photographer
what beauty he could possibly see.

5. Ferry Commuters, Staten Island, New York, 1944

Their four-minute eggs and quarrels
behind them, they head into the rest
of the day's opportunity and disappointment.
From our bird's-eye, we can make out
maybe five women in a wave of men, their backs to us
and pointed forward as the crow flies,
wearing business suits like coins
on their eyes for jobs or interviews.
Newspapers tucked routinely underarm,
most of the men sport "Bogie" fedoras,
as this was when cities were still walking towns.
Among the anonymity of darks and grays,
it matters less who the salesman or stenographer is,
who has forgotten to turn off the iron
or left a sick child at home,
who's even now looking to lunch before arriving
than that they were on time, are all aboard
and on with their undulating lives.

6. Grease Plant Worker, 1945

Except for a white curtain of roiling smoke,
everything seems so awfully dark,
from the scene's temporal parallel
with Sisyphus constantly atoning, to the boom
hoisting its barrel over a filthy platform,
to there at the heart of oblivion,
gathering another of his greasy burdens
for hauling to an appointed spot—
clad in what looks like a conductor's cap,
sooty leather apron and gauntlet—
the bootblack features of this fallen angel
lost in his sullen thought.

7. Farmer, Springfield, Connecticut, 1945

Much as how I remember my father,
this farmer seems tired, even weary perhaps,
after a short step, mopping his brow
in a pose that looks like crying or prayer.
His halted mares, one starred, satin black,
and to her far side, scarcely there,
a white harness mate slightly bowed,
pause in harmony on rough fescue.
Behind his team, whiffletree unhitched,
their wagon is silent and still,
waiting for loads or to be unloaded.
Above the low horizon, we can see
three leafing crowns of trees
spaced like Easter crosses,
and oh, what delicate cirrus clouds
fill the perfect, impenetrable ceiling.

8. Red Jackson, 1948

His sixteen-year-old mug
is that of a still green pugilist, pug-nosed,
sans the cauliflower ears, at least
from what we can tell
in this image hiding all else
but the luminescence through
a tenement's web of shattered glass
showing us bits of who he is
from the top of his matted head,
blazing his profile including cigarette
like a hot mask, helmet and visor,
then receding, then lighting nappy folds
of flannel shoulder and sleeve.
A likely scenario seems, Red,
without any of his Midtowners,
has almost stumbled across the turf
of rival war lords out in numbers,
and now holds on for an all clear
behind a flaking sash, wondering again
how much of his past is still before him
by the street's cold neon, a camera's steady flash,
his response to the *Life* photographer
who had asked to shadow him
blinking, "Ain't I got trouble enough?"

9. Harlem Rooftops, 1948

After the gloomy smokestacks
and shining pockets of steam
hovering near the composition's axis,
as if billowed through clefts over purgatory,
what one likely notices is an absence
of the possibility of buttercups. So far
removed from John Greenleaf Whittier's worlds
in which royal berries fall
across paths for barefoot boys,
is this gritty image where each life's story
seems screened behind small candles of glass,
where someone is trying to forget something
with someone else or to forget
someone else with something.
Even of darkened windows,
one wonders how sweet the broken sleep
of sirens could be, wonders about
the two or three shadowy mendicants
imagined in the bit of street shown below.
Still there is the brightness
of a few angles and edges,
and a gray, grainy sky
resting above like Vesuvian fire,
as are the hidden lofts
of murmuring pigeons.

10. Gang Member with Brick, 1948

If Rhodesian Man, who at some point
began to use fruits of his surroundings
for weapons, had existed, he might have
looked much like this rawboned southpaw,
without fedora of course, in rumpled
though modern togs, who also having guessed
another purpose for his opposable thumb,
squats among rubble in an alleyway
where a rich, sinister shadow slides
across the pockmarked wall of his slum.

11. Fight, 1948

Almost pirouetting, Red Jackson it seems,
has just missed with a wild haymaker
that nearly takes him to his knees
while his pompadoured opponent
on tiptoe, as if about to take flight,
has cocked a stabbing right
like an archer drawing his bow.
Blurred and overexposed, what an alien world this is
to the perfectly focused and posed shots
of a gold *Vogue* hourglass,
her perdition red lips, fingernails, and satin pumps
matched with tight *décolletage*
as she stands at a red doorway
in most flattering light, to lovers Bergman and Rossellini
in a small boat off the coast of Stromboli,
their stylish rainwear carelessly spattered,
to Miss Streisand in elaborate Dolly costume
against a lavish stage set of lavender blooms,
and especially to the white egret choir
perched on dark boughs of mimosa maybe
silhouetted by Prussian blue sky.
And yet here they are too,
part of the same collection, caught
with the same tool, these teen champions
from Harlem gangs, both in baggy secondhand trousers,
Red in plaid outing flannel shirt
and the opponent unbuttoned with sleeves
rolled up for work, now scuffling for life,
like the Hector and Achilles
that were being studied in some school.

12. Red Jackson and Herbie Levy Study Wounds on Face of Slain Gang
Member Maurice Gaines, 1948

So astonished and boyish now,
they've come to a dim parlor to view him—
to see *it*, to see if dead is like
what they had imagined,
whether their memories
of bragging about girls
or revenge on rival gangs,
whether anything of ease
could come to mind.
It's clear the undertaker
had done his best,
patching split lips,
restoring the swarthy complexion
from its bludgeoned rose,
draping that vapor of a body
in some man's handy suit,
even lending a bright, fragrant carnation
to the peaked lapel
like an Old Testament offering,
perhaps for a kind of sweet savor
so that any past sins
might be overlooked,
so that lying there
amid a taffeta cloud,
the mask of his face
seems as if nothing much
is really keeping him
from unfastening sanguine eyes,
rising up, and telling his friends
about one hell of a dream.

13. Death Room, Fort Scott, 1949

Of all his portraits of the elderly
waiting on the mercy of their Master,
this is most bitter by far
once our mind pans away from some
few pleasant, long ago moments
we fancy the wallpaper's
many morning glories having seen,
and down to our penultimate mystery
captured by values brightening
from weeds to winding-sheet
in a sorry trinity of hope.
Mrs. Jefferson, whom we know
from another photo of the same year,
sits bedside, her silvered head darkly netted
and her hollow, hallowed eyes
lifted to a realm of epiphany
in an undepicted corner
where Bethel appears
with shiny processions of angels
lining Jacob's ladder from heaven
to earth to heaven again.
In her wizened right hand,
the well-worn staff of other such pilgrimages,
as her all but audible hum
of chariots swinging sweetly low
wafts across yet another dead or dying sister
tucked and foreshortened in fetal ease,
this one's aged but still full face
with eyes closed and lips
slightly parted to let us know.
And the third figure,
also a woman on in years,
like Mrs. Jefferson, also in black topcoat,
stands at the foot and to the right of the bed,
her back to the lens, half in frame,
her graceful waves gently bowed in vigil,
most likely imagining twelve pearly ways
to a crystal stream and the tree beside
with its twelve manner of fruits
that will heal everything.

14. Uncle James Parks, Fort Scott, 1949

He sits there spectacled, hunched
to peer over the crook of his cane,
clearly ready for whatever else
that may happen to him—
drought or famine or pestilence,
the death of his last friend.
Garbed in old man's hat and clothes,
his profile shows there's little he hasn't seen,
though if not the Jardin des Tuileries of Paris,
certainly rabbit-tobacco and prince's plume
of Kansas in the spring, and if seldom
any peace that passeth
all understanding, then at least
in this instant before the shutter closes,
as he seems to be thinking
on a single, quiet thing.

15. Pool Hall, Fort Scott, 1949

Both building and sidewalk
are as grizzled as old beards,
as pitched as lean-tos,
but charming enough for five at least
who've gathered there this day,
from right to left, three casually posed
in an out of plumb doorway
while two older others
prop beside, and sit on, a near windowsill.
Among the grouping of three,
a short, middle-aged man
with an early paunch and light fedora,
is tilted in front of one
wearing hand-me-downs
who could be school-age still
and under cap a taller other
whose countenance is just hidden
by chiaroscuro. Of the two elder men
who look to be lifelong friends, who
a generation before, might've been
on that same threshold, now
the standing one with his dim crown
at a jaunty angle to match
two pieces of his suit,
his hands in the pockets of starched dungarees,
appears to be telling a story
that his buddy already knows
but patiently listens to, his own white brim
rolled in cowboy fashion
matched with swarthy dress coat,
faded overalls loosely cuffed and dull brogans,
plus cleverly turned to face the camera,
though checked by its leash,
his jet-black greyhound—
such a sleek, aristocratic beast.

16. Chicken Hawk, 1949

A dazzled hedge
of background greens
is blurred as savagery
sails in screaming
with all its weapons unsheathed.
Nearby, a ghost-white pullet
flaps the yard's panic
the same way our hens
and my mother used to
when they recognized
that high, baleful screech
in the seconds just before
its golden eye appeared
as wide and hot as the sun
from which it fell.

17. New England Countryside, 1949

A *mise en scène* of plump Holsteins
is herded to a weathered barn
for milking or evening by a fellow
who has guided this routine
thousands of times, so much so
that his head is down, his mind on other things,
as he follows over rocky outcroppings
through the ramshackle gap.
The farmer's nonchalant form,
even somewhat distant and clouded,
shows the paunch of his overalls,
his knee-high rubbers in stride.
Just as well though, as the cows also
look sleepy or distracted and have paused
to mull an off plumb doorway
they must've often passed before.
Across horizon and middle ground,
a pallor of ephemeral mist
shrouds all but ragged crests
of the highest trees, then gives way
to the foreground's untenable weeds.
Still, amid all this ruggedness,
there is a crude scallop
edging the barn roof's overhang
like a sign of amazing grace.

18. Benedictine Monastery, 1955

Each one's hood
bowed toward sacred text,
they stride single file
across a flurry of petals.
The seventh at the end
is at an angle to the rest,
quickly squaring his corner,
about to fall in line.
All we can see
from our perspective
are their stern silhouettes
against the patient landscape.
We can still tell
the wind is high
by a birch's driven branches
and the first brother's cowl
floating behind him
as though being lifted
by some invisible spirit.
Since there is no cloister
in our field of view,
we can only wonder if they
were headed there,
possibly at last,
for the blessing of speech.

19. Children at Play, Birmingham, Alabama, 1956

Poor shotgun homes
seem to be kept up
as best they can.
There are no calendulas
or violets for their yards,
not even wild onions or grass—
nothing but life-sapping clay
and a monstrous oak
with its Medusalike roots
creeping above ground;
so five small boys circle
the memory of a puddle
out in the clay road.
Four squat and one stands,
without puppies or dolls or marbles,
all connected yet each lost
in his own imagination,
while a slightly older boy
stands atop the big tree's roots,
staring at them for anything
different to happen, mesmerized,
waiting to be turned to stone.

20. Cotton Pickers, Alabama, 1956

O but what a perfect composition it is.
Twenty-two of them yet no two are so close
that we can't make out each woman or man.
It reminds one of Millet's *The Gleaners*—
those three sunburned peasants
gathering crumbs after some lord's scythe and wain.
Though under Millet's golden, sympathetic light,
the labor doesn't seem eternal, is bound to one spot,
while even the foreshortened Alabama rows
go on and on, from foreground almost into horizon.
A highlight on the lead woman's shoulder
means they are working in blood heat.
And the will of those loose dresses,
overalls, sun hats, and kerchiefs,
the arts of carrying a croker sack,
the way all are bowed so earnestly
before their next downy burden
are as if time is standing still.

21. Storefront, Alabama, 1956

Across a cobbled door,
the picture of a little blonde girl
whose life is nothing but cute frills,
rosy smile, and a well-buttered slice,
hails those who enter to
"Reach for Sunbeam Energy-Packed Bread."
Testaments to Camel cigarettes'
good flavor and mildness
are nailed to the small frame's
rough-hewn planks. A sign
saying "Thanks" and "Hurry Back!"
pasted in one window seems mostly
a curse of circumstance.
An old RC thermometer's arrow
points out sweltering heat.
Amid these idols of endorsement,
two mothers and six barefoot children
wait on a makeshift porch
like lepers at Bethesda,
while above on the gable,
the archangel Coca-Cola
hovers with its balm.

22. Drinking Fountains, Birmingham, Alabama, 1956

There like Tantalus starving beneath boughs of luscious fruit,
the little girl, a couple of steps ahead, gazes at posters of delights
outside storefront glass reflecting the witness of silhouetted trees.
Though everything is black or white, the innocent swirls
of strawberry ice cream for a quarter must have been
shocking pink, and the "Lickety Split" cornucopia of banana
and sauces a veritable rainbow for only ten cents more,
that butterscotch and Dairy Queen butter pecan
more golden than any honey in the Promised Land.
I've heard that Sibelius asked his grandchildren
for their dreams each morning, and if they said
they had dreamt of birds, he asked what kind of birds,
and if the birds had been singing, then what kind of songs.
With her gossamer back toward us, hand on hip
as she stands considering, while her lovely, obedient mother
stoops to "Colored Only" for the sparkling arc
that looks to be clean enough and possibly just as cold
as the one would be a few inches from its side,
we can but wonder if her dreams too hadn't been filled
by some melodious count before this heaven of days
when she and mama would parade alike,
lightly starched in their whitest finery
with the bliss of sweets on their lips, perhaps
stopping for a sip from either fount.

23. Willie Causey's Son with Gun during Violence in Alabama, 1956

Before their property was taken
and they were run out
of Choctaw County
under threat of a rope,
inside a corner room,
what looks to be mother
and two younger sons
bow bedside over an open book.
Mr. Causey's lank, elder boy,
perhaps even his first-born,
sits just outside without expression,
shirtless, barefoot,
wearing raggedy dungarees,
in a rickety chair
propped against the deep freezer.
Across his lap rests
an old bolt-action rifle
okay for squirrels and such,
but unlikely to get
more than one white man.

24. Flavio da Silva, Rio de Janeiro, 1961

When you look at him there
as skinny as nothing,
balancing himself with one leg raised
and crooked to cross the other
like a carnival trick, posing akimbo,
without one clean spot
on his tattered tee shirt and shorts,
you have to wonder how
his parents, José and Nair, kept dreaming
such lovely-sounding names.
Each time, eight times,
they come up with *Flavio*, as they used a hole
in their crumbling floor for a toilet;
Maria, while they suffered Flavio's
jaundiced, asthmatic coughing;
Mario, when they witnessed
the thumb-sucking hunger,
sores over arms and shins
multiply like those of Lazarus;
Luzia, amid the day's washing,
while Nair, her bare feet calloused and bleeding,
paused for a moment
under the shade of a jacaranda
near the base of their mountain;
Albia, as they heated what rice and beans
they could get hold of
atop a makeshift stove
cobbled from bricks and tin;
Isabel, maybe when they found
their children, flesh and blood,
siding like warring tribes against one another;
Baptista, after José returns
angry and weak from another long day
of peddling kerosene and bleach
for so few cruzeiros;
Zacarias, as they navigated the Catacumba,
which means "death" in Portuguese,
to their rotting favela

among the rotting favelados
packed like trash into a hillside,
or later, when Nair stirred
a little kerosene into some stale coffee
to calm Flavio's lungs;
and then perhaps, turning for a change
from their plague of ever-swarming flies
to just across that sparkling lagoon
separating them
from the palatial ways of the blessed,
for another already great
in the belly, waiting, unnamed.

25. Boy with June Bug, 1963

At his tender age
I too surely shared
that same sweet thought
in such beautiful, blinding, swirling mist
like the wonderfully diffused grasses
and pastel of blooms
framing this bit of profile
of his supine body,
just a little blue bib
vanishing into the lens's mesh
of shoulder and breast,
and the perfect submission
of his honey-colored face with eye
gently shut against the sun's stern light.
The farther elbow bent
to rise through background, his hand
dangles titanlike to slender fingers
smudged with good earth,
forefinger and thumb pinching
a strand of yarn
holding fast but pulled taut
by the five free legs of a lustrous beetle
frozen on its captor's still forehead.
Here he lies
as if waiting out wars
and rumors of wars,
perhaps not even dreaming
of the whirligig he's tamed, not mindful
of the midge or seed on his cheek,
nor of what others
have said he should become,
but of how fine this feels now,
perhaps of some plumping berry patch
or cool secluded pond.

26. Color Gallery

When you turn to color, you give us
a little blue Peruvian girl
that could be from the hand
of Velázquez, or perhaps in some ways
even Picasso's, as she stands
never having reason to have learned
how to pose, looking almost cornered
against a crazed, cerulean wall;
a still early, but perfect circle
of yellow sun glinting across the morning orange
of your *Western Dawn*, as a cowboy astride his alert mount
herds silhouettes of cattle through dust rising
more like smoke from flame;
that solitary dove which you must have seen
a figure of eternity in since you veiled it
in ethereal light, superimposing your crystalline will
to bestow an archaic, lichenous effect
to properly white plumage, to the velvet darkness
as bird stares downward, deific, perching
on something we can't see or comprehend.
There is your swirl of brilliantly golden eels
molded like an ancient bracelet,
or like Ouroboros spiraled head to tail
as if ready to swallow itself
and then miraculously begin anew.
As for the lovely nudes, what is there to say?
We want them, just as you intended—
the fantastic girl's silkiness and slender shoulders,
her tan fingers caressing the hush
of her throat, lying entranced, supine,
on the luminous, alabaster shore
of your dreamscape beach, amid
mountainous scallop and conch shells,
her hair flowing as if being rinsed in the sand,
making her seem even more akin to the waves;
and the shell pink form of a geisha in repose,
she turning from us to gaze
through a portal onto the new sunrise

of what appears to be a virgin time and place,
but is actually your *Western Dawn* again
sixteen years later, reused here for background.
And there's the mystery of what they
might really be thinking off in canticle,
cloaked in their crisp habits, these Parisian nuns.
There's the New York still life
of a polished mahogany writing desk
with all its warm accoutrements
of gilded, leather-bound volumes,
wire-rimmed spectacles marking an open book,
pocket watch and pipe, the embossed cup
filled with neatly sharpened pencils,
the bric-a-brac of ceramic ducks,
a bronze boot and such,
with just enough documents and correspondence
stacked ever so casually precise, that arty flourish
of a raven's quill dipped in elegant inkwell,
while on the shelf above the hutches,
a small baroque clock and one's shiny letter opener
wait among ghostly daguerreotypes. Ghostly because
the photographer's subjects were probably long since dead,
just as so many of yours are—
surely the old woman hunched under
a black umbrella, feebly carrying her burgundy pocketbook
through the 1950 streets of Paris; and the Sicilian peasant
whose shock of umber veins rose like oak roots
up through her rough, tired hands;
and that phantom leopard beside
a shimmering blue pool in Brazil, 1962;
and now even you, the second half of your autumn
and finally winter too having come and gone.
Though not without leaving us all this
of your world to behold, especially new wonders
you announced as "recent work"—these images
having become much less about earth.
For example, the corolla of white petals
only blushed with a touch of this life
appears to be ascending into powder blue sky,
and in another, infinitely white crepe paper,

shaded and backlit, is gracefully crumpled
and pinched into what could be clouds,
or even a choir of angels swirled around
the wisp of a budding branch
literally out of electric blue grace,
all beneath some blank button or toy
that you no doubt happened upon
to use as your bright, constant moon.
But with these symbols of tranquility and reward
are the equally beautiful—though frighteningly so—
descents into burned netherworlds,
a paradise lost as it were,
like the wondrously rugged, yet incredibly sheer
myth of a land in which something huge, lepidopteran,
torn from darkest cloth, hovers above a glowing abyss.
Similarly, a frail bridge is barely swung
over the plunge between pitch-black cliffs
shrouded in thick, sulfurous mist.
Most anxious of all are those dusky shucks
of some passed life cast into the tattered
soullike thing endlessly wandering
through torrents of ochre and blue.
And then as epilogue perhaps,
the soft rhythm of an image called *Moonscape*
wafts over us as well as your creation
of a calm, crestlit sea reflecting your deep utterance
that "only the moon really knows me."

IV. *Effets de Neige*

Looking at Blackbirds

Watching my own legion
of autumn blackbirds
swoosh and light, as loud
and synchronized as ever,
one week before
another birthday, I dream mostly
about how washed in blue
the sky appears, about
how the stars will twinkle
on what promises to be
such a clear night,

or maybe not
actually twinkle, but tremble
maybe like this time of year's
violet shadows that scatter
through windows,
shimmer across cabinets
and floors,

tremble like the twitch
I've noticed in old men's thumbs,
which they say
may come and go,
or stay, or get worse,

or tremble even
as if the stars themselves
have grown weak
after millennia
to now flickering bulbs.

As for the birds,
although I've never
harmed them, they still flush
from the slightest creak
of a door being
opened or closed.

What was it Stevens
named that moment
when he looked out
the way we often do
at the so beautiful world
and begin thinking
of other disparate things,
when he imagined the metaphor
and rhyme of their flight?

Ah yes, "a small part
of the pantomime."

Swift Transition

Half an hour earlier,
        a smiling woman had asked
                if I were enjoying
                        our splendid fall weather,

and of course
        I was, till later
                while driving home
                        beyond town, when easy

and just in front of me,
        out of freshly
                rusted thickets
                        into the gloriously blue,

stole red-tailed hawk,
        and gathered like golden
                a plump wood rat
                        kicking slight semaphore,

off across the road
        to some leafy last
                sequestering. Off
                        unless spared

by a benevolent stalk,
        if any among lespedeza
                or thistle
                        can strike to redeem

from the talon
        of this winged thing
                that, even in our
                        most beautiful days,

swoops one away,
      and otherwise lights
            in grim enjambment
                  over the yet winding heart
to strip rosy
      necessities
            like Atropos snipping
                a string.

Memento Mori

after paintings by Andrew Wyeth

1. Christina's World

The girl doesn't seem a girl,
but the memory
or dream of a girl.
Wyeth himself claimed Christina
could have been left out
and the painting
would've remained the same,
that her physical presence
was no more important
than a beached lobster's
or anything else's in one
of his many other watercolors,
that her essence was bound
in a toy-blue sky,
in the sweep of earth tone fields.

So you may think,
what a thing to say about
such a once starry-eyed spirit,
especially if you've gazed
into her haggish, glintless portrait
he did a mere twenty years later.
Maybe you too sorrowed
for the absence
of her slender youth,
her fascination with
the pepper of crows
sifting from a barn's loft,
with a weathered farmhouse
also on the distant horizon,
as she lies in our foreground,
her then lithe body
halfway between tucked and prone.

Not mindful of the meals
that will always
need to be cooked,
linen that will need
to be washed and aired,
eggs to be gathered
and chickens fed,
with her back to the rest of us,
it's as if she somehow understands
that she should hold
this moment, alone, for as long
as she possibly can.

2. Tenant Farmer

There's much
about the strict gables
and high chimneys,
its crumbling courses
of sooty brick
and small, dark panes
that say this
wasn't a house of apologies.

Love was stark,
measured in provisions.
And so another day
white under snow,
still gray with more,
there seem to be
enough backlogs sawn
to stoke fires for a while.

With no crops
to be grown or gathered
in hard weather,
with what little work
that could be done,
there were surely
parsnips and tomatoes
canned in the cellar,
wild jams lining shelves
in the old lean-to,

and for any debt
that had to be paid
in kind this winter,
strung plumb by her neck
over the naked limb of a willow
a coldly rendered doe.

3. Spruce Bough

Just a small delight
of the natural world,
yet it's as if I'm being reborn
to my earlier life,
and again love that
we aren't supposed to be
able to see between
thick veils of needles
on a snow-laden bough,
but where all the same
I can imagine daring
such cold, dark washes
of background color,
someway weaving
around, beneath,
till somehow inside, following
the commerce of faith
to find all the bright gardens
of this and that
kind of bird.

Effets de Neige

1. The Banks of the Marne in Winter

       after a painting by Camille Pissarro

The painter calls it *winter*. Most would say
it's too green to be a time of dying.
No sullen flocks fill the skies with their crying.
Where is the struggling peasant, the decay?
A field by the road looks like a spring ley.
Émile Zola wrote Pissarro's trying
failed beauty, but there was no denying
it was dark and austere in the right way.
On that road two figures, adult and child,
are headed to or away from their home,
as there are some pleasant hillside houses
in sight, and while the weather still seems mild
enough to make it, a gathering dome
of clouds warn all that winter arouses.

2. Hunters in the Snow

after a painting by Gustave Courbet

What scent has one's tethered, straining dog found
so necessary that he must get to,
determined now to search a windrow through?
Perhaps he has picked up the muffled sound
of frightened heartbeats crouched on frozen ground.
The dog's eagerness seems to be a clue
that caching game will break cover, then do
what is hoped for by both hunters and hound,
unless it's merely some other dog's trail,
a pungent beacon that he can't resist,
and for the moment, luck spares grouse or hare.
Maybe these hunters twigged by their dog's tail,
it's just the spot where another dog pissed
and are yanking his leash to try elsewhere.

3. Snow at Louveciennes

     after a painting by Alfred Sisley

The earlier of Sisley's winter scenes
is more hushed, while the second seems more still
and urgent a test of his figure's will.
Both are titled *Snow at Louveciennes*,
but the latter's undulant brushwork means
to add something to the bluish gray chill
of heavy, threatening sky. There's no shrill
squeal of any child playing. Sharp wind keens
for whatever may have been wrong inside,
or so it might look to our viewer's eye
from the way the chemin de l'Etarché
is closing in on one woman. A tide
of thick snow filling the street leads us nigh,
though what has brought her out, we just can't say.

4. January: Cernay, near Rambouillet

after a painting by Léon Germain Pelouse

A carillon of birds hangs in the air
under orange clouds heavy with more snow.
Sky and field seem lit by a holy glow,
as do roofs, chimneys, and the white trees there,
hence such beautiful stillness everywhere.
Only those dark nets of birds have to go
some place. All else are in house or burrow.
We can nearly hear hearth fires crack and flare
while everything waits for the freeze to end,
for the yet distant purple of crocus
as a sign of beating mortality,
surviving whatever the heavens send
like that flock of cold voices in chorus
remembering spring's radiant mercy.

5. The Red Cape

after a painting by Claude Monet

First, we wonder why the woman looks sad
while she stands in snow gazing back inside
as if there were words someone should have tried
to put better, or the weather seemed bad.
Perhaps she's thinking of a life she had
long dreamt of but had always been denied—
those eyes doubly cold, saying she has plied
this path before. Though what if she is glad
of cozy rooms that await her return
as she glances through the open curtain,
her cadmium red scarf carefully tight?
Maybe there's something she just can't discern,
some jot of which she is still uncertain
like whether she is posed exactly right.

6. The Magpie

after a painting by Claude Monet

This is not a winter of discontent
though the crackled paint reminds us of age,
but what the French have called *effet de neige*—
just the absoluteness of a moment
before its mauve and pink fiction is spent
and a magpie's black, white, and blue message
vanishes with the haste of a turned page
defying the artist's eye and intent.

We're left questioning whether bird remained
centered on a gate for him to complete
and then *en plein air* capture snow still bright,
amazed that fence shadows wouldn't have changed
too quickly to be done *sur le motif*
against the world's constantly failing light.

7. Frost

after a painting by Claude Monet

How secret and primeval this grove seems
and how cold it has been made to appear.
By the jingle of white strokes we can hear
a frozen chime of branches. The scene gleams
as we might expect to see when one dreams
of such isolation. There's the slight fear
that lands with a bird's flutter, scrapes of deer
hidden among those red, brown, and blue themes
of abstraction, apparent solitude.
A path of green dashes that look like tracks
sink quickly across impasto snow.
Here Monet also chooses to include
an old sled under bowed trees where ice cracks,
clashes, in beauty that feels like zero.

Looking at Photos of Poets Grown Old

Looking at photos of poets grown old,
we envy the bacchic nights in Paris.
From their faces, many stories unfold,

and yet we know so much remains untold,
present there in the still twinkled iris.
Looking at photos of poets grown old

in drab clothes, out of fashion, what we hold
are lovely lines about Buenos Aires.
From their faces, many stories unfold

with creeping crow's-feet, missing teeth, flesh rolled
softly over the murmur of wildness.
Looking at photos of poets grown old,

we recall aspens brightening to gold
through the thin, frosted hair now more careless.
From their faces, many stories unfold

like revisions meticulously scrolled
as new mythology for us in this
looking at photos of poets grown old.
From their faces, many stories unfold.

Schubert's Wish

I wonder if it was raining as Franz Schubert lay
listening to Beethoven's String Quartet in C sharp minor,
as it was when I first heard it, if Schubert had also imagined
the opening movement as wistfully and wrong as I,
that it should start with an ethereal flutter of strings—
perhaps the petal spiraling from a flown bluebird
down through honeygold light of a late winter evening—
or somehow come upon us, dazzling like the Pentecostal fire
of morning across a field of frost. Anyway,
from the very beginning, an adagio sounds as if
it's already disappearing, as if one's mode of transport
already boarded, saying goodbye, but more like
a ship setting sail than my bird in flight.

The funny thing is, just a few years earlier,
he had accused Beethoven's art of being bizarre,
stirring wild passions instead of leading listeners to God.
Even so, it seems, as in Eliot's *Four Quartets*,
Schubert wants to hear less of men's wisdom
and more of their folly. For when on his deathbed,
he longs to hear even the master's *sul ponticello*,
known in its much worldlier sense as bowing
the sounds of "rats' feet on broken glass."

In that delirium of one's last requests
for sweets tasted from childhood, to stroke
an old photograph again—or like my father
near the end, in a kind of penitence I guess,
wanting me around always—Schubert chooses passage
on the gentle scherzos, the trills, directions
and notes scribbled over the room's glazed air,
till through the stormy finale, where, if anything, it all
seems less triumphant than maybe hoped for or expected,
unsettlingly quick, like the sound of a circle closing.

The author offers grateful acknowledgment to the following publications, in which some of the poems herein originally appeared, sometimes in a different form:

African American Review: "Fight, 1948," "Flavio da Silva, Rio de Janeiro, 1961," "Pool Hall, Fort Scott, 1949," "Uncle James Parks, Fort Scott, 1949"

Euphony: "Christina's World," "Tenant Farmer"

Image: "Death Room, Fort Scott, 1949," "Deus ex Machina," "Early Morning on the B Line from Vero Beach to Orlando after a Poetry Festival," "The Egret Tree," "Meadow Flowers (Goldenrod and Wild Aster)"

Killens Review of Arts and Letters: "Gang Member with Brick, 1948," "Harlem Rooftops, 1948," "Red Jackson, 1948"

Poem: "Before Waking," "Benedictine Monastery, 1955," "The Blood of Birds," "Ferry Commuters, Staten Island, New York, 1944," "Learning to Swim," "Mid-May"

Southern Quarterly: "American Gothic, 1942," "Boy with June Bug, 1963," "Children at Play, Birmingham, Alabama, 1956," "Cotton Pickers, Alabama, 1956," "Drinking Fountains, Birmingham, Alabama, 1956," "Snowy Egret Flies over Parched Mississippi Field," "Storefront, Alabama, 1956," "Willie Causey's Son with Gun during Violence in Alabama, 1956"

Vermont Literary Review: "The Garden of Allah"

Xavier Review: "Farmer, Springfield, Connecticut, 1945," "New England Countryside, 1949"

photo by Ellen E. Fischer

Claude Wilkinson is a critic, essayist, painter, and poet. His previous poetry collections include *Reading the Earth*, winner of the Naomi Long Madgett Poetry Award, and *Joy in the Morning*, which was nominated for a Pulitzer Prize. He has served as the John and Renée Grisham Visiting Southern Writer in Residence at the University of Mississippi. Other honors for his poetry include a Walter E. Dakin Fellowship and the Whiting Writers' Award. He lives in Nesbit, Mississippi.

CPSIA information can be obtained
at www.ICGtesting.com
Printed in the USA
LVHW03s2228070918
589486LV00001BA/4/P